DOUBLED RADIANCE

POETRY & PROSE
OF LI QINGZHAO

Translated by

KAREN AN-HWEI LEE

Acknowledgements

Cover Art

Image Number: CARP07672
Accession Number: 1919.483
Artist: Unknown
Title: Katagami Textile Stencil with Flowing Chrysanthemum Design
Date: Late Edo-Meiji period, 19th-early 20th century
Medium/Support: Chûban (medium-sized) minogami (mulberry bark paper) treated with persimmon juice and cut using the "tsukibori" (thrust-carving) technique, with "ito-ire" (silk-web) reinforcement
Dimensions: paper: H. 32.1 x W. 43.6 cm (12 5/8 x 17 3/16 in.)
Pattern Unit: H. 19.7 x W. 35.8 cm (7 3/4 x 14 1/8 in.)
Credit Line: Harvard Art Museums/Arthur M. Sackler Museum, Gift of Dr. Denman W. Ross, 1919.483
Photo: Imaging Department
© President and Fellows of Harvard College

Library of Congress Control
Number: 2017941768

ISBN-10: 0-933439-15-6
ISBN-13: 978-0-933439-15-3

Singing Bone Press
Singingbonepress.com

The task of the translator
is to facilitate this love between the original and its
shadow, a love that permits fraying....

Gayatri Chakravorty Spivak

I hear spring is especially beautiful this year,
doubled radiance of flowers and moonlight.

Li Qingzhao

Table of Contents

PREFACE

A coincidence. Seeking a rare vision of grace in the ash of war, exile, and a ruined economy, my eye fell upon a Song Dynasty woman poet's writings via an ideogram shared by our last names: 李. As far as equivalencies between our languages, her last name and mine are one and the same.

Her full name: Li Qingzhao.

As a girl, I knew about the Tang Dynasty male poet Li Bai or Li Po, whose famous poem on moonlight I memorized and recited. I was new to a woman poet named Li. I found Li Qingzhao while perusing Dorothy Disse's on-line archive, *Other Women's Voices: Translations of Women's Writing before 1700.* Romanized, Li Qingzhao's beautiful surname is also spelled Ching-ch'ao.

For Anglophone tongues, the third syllable is close to "ts" in "tse-tse fly."

Li adored her husband Zhao Mingcheng, who shared her literary interests. Li was perpetually in love with Zhao. They collected art and played "poetry games." After composing a line or identifying a quotation, the winner drank a cup of tea, which Li occasionally spilled on herself, laughing aloud. She took pleasure in book-collecting, observing chrysanthemums and pear blossoms, or sitting quietly with a burning censer after dusk. Li wrote original poems set to the tune of popular songs called *ci*.

Lyrical and passionate, her work stands apart from Song Dynasty women who chose to write stylized verse framed by imperial culture. At once intimate and universal, Li voices a timeless reality: Love, memory, and loss are integral to human experience. Indeed, her life of writing and art-collecting was doomed by the political instabilities of her time. After the fall of the Northern Song Dynasty, she and Zhao fled into exile as their possessions were reduced to ash.

As a translator, my desire is for Li's voice to sing in these translations.

She recalls a youthful boating excursion with joy, observes a courtyard plantain tree flourish in her southern exile, listens to rain on the leaves of a parasol tree, watches for the first signs of yellow chrysanthemums, or alludes to her late husband with tender regret while her own hair silvers at the temples. Her solitude is quite transparent in a reference to the mythic *peng* bird who soars on wind over water for ninety thousand *li*.

Doubled Radiance

Rumeng ling, No. 1: As if a reverie

Often remember
a pavilion by the stream at dusk, when
delirious with wine, we lost our route.
High spirits waned as our boat turned late
through a dense patch of fragrant lotus.
Oaring and oaring through, rowing,
we startled a flock of shore birds.

lighthearted
even though they were
lost.

Rumeng ling, No. 2: As if a reverie

Last night, a strong wind drove sparse rain;
deep slumber failed to thin the wine.
At daybreak, I queried the screen-rolling servant,
who replied: *Why, the crabapple tree is as always.*
Don't you see, don't you see?
How the foliage is robust green
yet floral redness, thin frailty.

lots of green. not
a lot of apples?

Huan xi sha, No. 1: Sands of a silk-washing stream

Don't let the wine cup flow with lion-hued amber.
Sadness overflows, settles without the onset of wine
as distant chimes ring quietly in the late evening wind.

Incense, a diminishing fragrance, breaks a dream
and my little gold hairpins loosen their clasp
     as I open my eyes
to a burning candle's shower of flame-blossoms,
red–embered happiness.

dreams

Huan xi sha, No. 2: Sands of a silk-washing stream

Spring's deep core rests in the small courtyard window;
unrolled screens cast darkening shades;
upstairs, in wordless solitude, I strum my jasper lute.

A distant mountain range thins the falling dusk;
silken wind, rain-blown, sends faint shadows in motion
as ineluctable pear blossoms, withering, wilt to fade.

Huan xi sha, No. 3: Sands of a silk-washing stream

On this quiet spring day
of fireless remembrance,
when curled wisps of incense rise cooled
from a drowned jade burner, extinguished,
a dream returns, journeying
to the hill-pillow over my flowered hairpins.

When migrant sea swallows are yet to arrive,
when men and women play at naming grasses,
when riverside plum flowers pass maturity
and willows bear catkins,
a soft light rain of yellow autumn
      soaks the lone garden swing.

loneliness to her
melancholy

Huan xi sha, No. 4: Sands of a silk-washing stream

Saddened by the last days of spring,
    I fail to brush my hair
as plum petals drift in our courtyard
    with evening wind.
Sparse clouds come and go,
    and soft moonlight is thinning.

Camphor incense cools in a jade bird-shaped vessel.
A drawn vermilion canopy hides its red tassels;
not even a bright rhinoceros horn will dispel the cold.

too sad to take care of herself.

Huan xi sha, No. 5: Sands of a silk-washing stream

Upstairs, on this clear spring day,
green shades are shut on four sides.
Before the house, perfumed grasses
merge with sky and water's edge.
Pray a government official
will fail to ascend to the top rung.
New shoots crowd the hall
under a bamboo grove.
Spring petals are falling,
swallows build mud nests;
in solitude, I endure sounds
of a stirring woodland,
the sylvan cry
of a lone cuckoo.

Tanpo huan xi sha, No. 1: Long variation on sands
  of a silk-washing stream

Ten thousand gold petals, light and frail, caressed;
blue-tinted jade leaves gently trimmed and layered.
Indeed, this flower has the spirit and grace of Yen Fu,
his marvelous genius.

Flowering plum hearts are common, by far;
lowly perfumed lilacs, a thousand times bittersweet.
Yet this rare fragrance penetrates my solace-laden
        dreams of one thousand *li*
        utterly without compassion.

Zhegu tian, No. 1: A partridge sky for the cassia flower

Yellow lightness, soft and exquisite,
sparse elegance, reserved in manner,
you secrete potent perfume.
Why favor emerald and vivid red?
One yellow flower reigns over all.

Plum blossoms are envious
while chrysanthemums, ashamed:
Our cassia flower crowns the display
at autumn's grand opening.
Poets writing in the style of Qu Yuan
are bereft of true inspiration, graceless
not to have discovered the cassia years ago.

Yujia ao, No. 1: A fisherman's pride

The snow carries a letter from spring
as winter plum flowers adorn jade-smooth branches,
their fragrant, delicate, half-open faces trembling
in the midst of a courtyard's winter scene,
lovely as a young woman arising from her bath.

Perhaps creation was stirred by inspiration
to instruct the clear bright moon
in gently rendering the earth's translucence.
So let us sip green-ants wine in cups of gold,
and let us not delay intoxication
with a flower whose beauty is far beyond compare.

Huangdi ge (shi): The emperor's chamber

Eminent as the sun and moon in the heavens,
illustrious as the reigns of emperors Yao and Xun,
true as a celestial compass points north, unwavering,
the fame of your vast imperial armies
is recorded with high praise in the chronicles.
Elegant mats woven of yellow gold,
even mythical jade couches are flawed gifts.
The courtyard glows with fragrant torches
in the spring wind, shining effulgence.
Don't light the perfumed incense yet.

Guifei ge (shi): Imperial consort's chamber

A gold bracelet is your token of honor,
like Gou Yi in the resplendent palace.
Spring is born in your canopied bed
of blue cypress seeds
where the emperor drinks ecstasy
lasting a thousand years.

a lot of
thnk what
the reasons

Jianzi mulanhua: Short version of the magnolia

Out of the florist's shoulder baskets,
I bought one spring branch
on the verge of blooming,
<u>tear-stained</u> lightness
of blushing clouds, sunrise dew.
Afraid my beloved will say
my face is not comely as the blossoms
aslant in my hair, cirrus at the temples,
I dare him to look and compare.

Attributed to Li Qingzhao

thin white clouds

still look @ me even though I am aging

Chang Tzu says go w/ the flow, don't get attached

13

Xiari jue ju (shi): Broken lines under a summer sun

After birth, one should strive for heroism,
surviving in memory after death.
Today, we reflect upon brave Xiang Yu
who refused to flee across the east river.

Qing qingchao man: Celebrating a slow luminous dawn

A low drape veils the women's quarters.
Carved banisters guard your solitary stance
in the fading spring, alone on the terrace.
Your light floral presence is like water.
Your purity radiates natural charm.
You persist when other flowers vanish,
adorning yourself in wind, dew, and dusk.
Spirit of spring desires you
with covetous winds, moonlit laughter.
A persevering sun rises
above the eastern side of the city,
the south side's rice field paths,
a lake inn basking in direct light,
and perfumed wheels turning swiftly.
A sumptuous feast disperses ephemera.
Who will follow in your fragrant dust?
Brighter than a resplendent palace,
dawn breaks through your budding arms.
As gold vessels pour wine
against the dimness of a flickering candle,
I envy not the yellow dusk.

This person
is irreplacable

Seasons come + go, a person
can go but never come back

Ti bayonglou (shi): Composed for the tower
  of eight poems

A thousand classical winds
praise the tower of eight poems;
sentinel mountains, scenic rivers
grieve the poet's loss.
Three thousand *li* of waters
course through the south,
vigilance for river glens
in fourteen counties.

Su zhong qing: Pouring out my heart

Intoxicated late at night,
I pulled my hair ornaments slowly,
plum petals on a dry branch.
Odor of wine broke my spring reverie; I woke, *likes her*
fractured dreams failed to return. — *dreams alot?*
Now everything is somber.
Moonlight lingers.
Green drapes, closed.
I caress the remnant petals.
I coax their last perfume.
And now, I recall the moments, demurring.

Tiren jiao: A beautiful woman at leisure
for the plum blossoms in the rear pavilion

Fragile jade, fragrant sandalwood,
alone through the deep snow drifts,
my soul burns in the annual search
for late-blooming plum flowers.
In your upper room at the river inn,
clouds spill over an expanse of water.
I languish an eternity in this fair setting,
loiter against the railing, lowered aqua blinds.
A guest arrives. With full cups of wine,
we sing together, yet water never ceases
overflowing until it touches the clouds.
Southern plum branches need trimming.
Let's not wait until echoes
    of a nomad's flute
emerge from the western chamber.

18

Duoli, yong baiju: Quite beautiful,
   white chrysanthemum song

The little chamber is cold tonight.
Blinds are lowered in the long darkness.
I despise clattering rain and loveless wind;
at night, they ruin the pale jade skin
   of white chrysanthemums.
Unlike Gui Fei's intoxicated, florid countenance,
or Sun Shou's sad, shapely eyebrows,
Han Ling who received a gift of stolen incense,
and the woman from Xu who used facial powder,
none surpasses the rare blossom's novelty.
Let us examine the chrysanthemum to see
whether Qu Yuan and Tao Ling's poetic styles
suit the flower. A soft wind rises,
sending fine perfume, a summer rose.
When autumn ends gradually,
this snow-pure, jade-thin flower
is loathe to part from companions
like the sad young women in Han Gao
   who surrendered their jade ornaments,
or tears scattered on a white silk fan
   graced with a poem by Ban Zhao.
Whether in moonlight, fresh wind, or dark
   rain and fog,

19

the skies cause flowers to wilt
and their perfumed silhouettes vanish.
Even love cannot know
how long they're loaned to us.
Perhaps if we had the best intentions,
we wouldn't need to remember the flowers
by the riverside and east chrysanthemum hedge.

wldent
nave them
forever

in a dereret
nwrd you wardnt
nave to remember
themso vividly
bc they wandet
be there forever

Better to have
love than lost
them not to
have love @ all.

Lin jiang xien, No. 1: Immortals gaze at the river

The courtyard rests in secluded depth,
rooms and windows clouded by mist:
   spring is late this year.
For whose sake has my fragrant air wilted?
Luminous dreams of you come with night.
All the southern trees must be in bloom.

Delicate jade or lightweight sandalwood,
   pure love is free of antipathy.
A nomad's flute in the southern chamber
   should cease playing:
Don't you know the flute's song will disperse
   the rich aroma of perfume?
Warm wind sidles through lengthening days,
   and we'll be apart
until the apricot flowers are in full bloom.

[handwritten annotation: The seasons leaving many. She has to leave behind what she loves.]

21

Dian jiang chun: Applying lip rouge

Sequestered in the women's chamber, I sense
a thousand strands of sorrow
    sewn into an inch of my spirit.
To adore spring is to see spring leave
as light rain impels the flight of petals.
Restless, I lean over the balustrade,
the end of my intricate skein of desire.
Where is the one I love?
Only the skies touch dry perfumed grasses,
cutting off the path of his return.

[handwritten annotation:] To adore spring is to see spring leave you dont know what you have till its gone

Zuihua ying: Intoxicated by floral shadows

Thin fog, dense clouds, day-length sorrow;
camphor incense vanishes from a gold burner.
It's the Chong Yang season, a chrysanthemum festival.
On my jade cushion, through the light silk bed-curtain,
    midnight chill prevails.

At the east hedge, I hold cups of wine
    until yellow dusk.
Darkness, a perfume, fills my sleeves.
Never say this moment dispels vertigo
when rolled blinds move in the west wind,
and a woman is thinner than a yellow flower.

Pusa man, No. 1: A religious foreigner

Gentle wind and early spring sunshine
mean a light dress, sense of warmth
though I felt chilled on waking --
a plum flower wilted in my hair.
Drinking wine helps with forgetting.
While I slept, the incense lost its glow,
    bereft of fragrance,
yet the burning wine still flowed.

Does she want to forget?
or to remember
her husband

Pusa man, No. 2: A religious foreigner

With strong cries, wild swans
　　break the blue-tinted clouds;
snow falls and smoke rises outside my window;
under the candle, my phoenix hairpin glitters;
a silhouetted hair ornament weighs little;
a sounding trumpet ushers in the dawn
whose rising colors push back the night,
　　dark herds of cattle;
still, it is hard to contemplate spring flowers
when the west wind is cold, bitter as usual.

She doesn't
like the
cold.

Hard to think
about the flowers

Xing xiangzi, No. 1: Fragrance in motion

Dazzling autumn skies, open radiance
against dark contortions of grief.
I search for gold chrysanthemums,
signs of the Chong Yang festival.
Putting on a light dress,
sipping new green-ants wine,
I sense a fickle wind arise,
changing into a little rain,
then a slight chill.

Yellow dusk covers the yard.
Disconsolate, I sleep off the wine,
my spirit choked with sorrow.
Enduring the deep night alone,
moonbeam on our empty bed,
I listen to the rhythmic washing
of clothes on a laundry stone,
the little sounds of crickets,
and endless dripping water.

Xiaochong shan: Little mountains

Lush spring grass at the door,
red plum flowers burst open,
still not uniformly in bloom.
A jar adorned with blue-tinted clouds,
    jade crushed into ash
as dawn sends remnants of a dream
to break open a small cup of spring.
Floral shadows press heavily on the gate.
Pale moonlight touches a sparse screen
    with yellow twilight.
For two years, you've left me for the east
three times. Please return soon:
Our ecstasy will surpass the spring.

Is spring a metaphor for her husband?

27

Wuling chun: Wuling spring

Fragrant petal-scented dust:
When flowers vanish
and wind ceases late in the day,
I am too tired to brush my hair.
Household objects are unchanged,
but with my beloved's absence,
all quotidian matters cease.
Silent tears are prelude
to the flow of speech.

I've heard about the beauty
of coupled rivers in springtime
and plan on sailing
my light boat there.
I'm concerned, though,
this little grasshopper boat
cannot float the burden of grief.

Yuan wangsun, No. 1: Lament for the prince

Water drops quietly broke my dream.
With dense sorrows unsettled by wine,
I arose from a cold jeweled pillow,
opened aqua-colored screens to dawn,
and wondered who swept
all traces of dry red petals.
Night wind, perhaps.

Song of a jade flute ends,
and the flutist vanishes like spring.

I endure our trials of separation
bitter and resentful
against this passion, this regret,
this prolonged torment.
I inquire of traveling clouds
the whereabouts
of my beloved in the east.

Attributed to Li Qingzhao

Asks the sky where her husband is

29

Fenghuang tai shang yi chui xiao:
Playing the flute on the phoenix terrace, a memory

Chilled incense rests in its gold burner,
my quilt overturned in red waves.
Slowly I rise in the morning to comb my hair.
A mirror of precious stones fills with dust,
the rising sun mounts our curtain hooks,
and I fear the bitter pain of our separation.
So close to sharing my heart, I can't speak.
I am thinner lately, wasting away
not from wine illness,
not from seasonal grief or autumn sadness.
Cease, cease –
This time, my love, when you left me,
not a thousand, ten thousand Yang Guan
songs of departure could restrain you.
Now remembering you, my Wuling beloved,
when fog shuts me inside my Qing chamber,
when only the water flowing before our residence
returns my solitary gaze, one lasting through the day,
I focus unwaveringly on that moment,
adding yet another length of sorrow.

She stares off the whole day thinking of the moment he found at.

Xing xiangzi, qi xi, No. 2: Fragrance in motion,
   seven dusks

Evening crickets chirp in the grass
while leaves drop from the parasol tree,
startling. This season of sorrow
intensifies on earth as in heaven.
Clouds are stairways, moonlight is earth,
yet our way is sealed by a thousand locks.
If floating rafts were to journey
between sea and sky, still
never would the two meet.

A star-laden bridge made by magpies
for one annual tryst recalls in heaven
the trials of our separation, endless regrets:
A cattle hand and weaver maiden, in love,
face to face once a year on the celestial bridge.
Perhaps this is why, with our partings,
our emotions clear for only an instant,
followed by sudden rain,
sudden wind.

31

Sheng sheng man: Slow musical notes

Searching and searching,
chilled, empty, and saddened –
Quick warmth shifts once more to winter
when peace eludes my resting place.
Two or three small cups of diluted wine
cannot dispel the chill evening wind.
Migrant geese, messenger birds in flight
grieve my broken heart,
feathered friends passing from another time.
Now the earth is heaped with yellow petals
disarrayed, ruined. Who'll pick them up?
Sitting at the window,
how do I alone prevail against darkness?
When a fine rain falls on the parasol tree,
dripping quietly through a yellow dusk,
when I consider all things in this very moment,
one word, sorrow, utterly fails.

Cant put it
into words bc
words arent adequate
for what shes
felings

Yi jianmei: One cut plum flower branch

Fragrant traces of red lotus
    linger autumnal on my jade mat.
Gently I unfasten my silk clothes
in solitude aboard the orchid boat.
Who sends a brocaded letter through the clouds?
Messenger birds return this season, writing their flight
across a full moon over the western chamber.

By nature, petals drift in the wind, and water flows.
One kind will cling to its own:
In two places, though, with sorrows of leisure
    spent apart,
mourning descends my brow
only to climb aboard my heart.

Die lian hua, No. 1: Butterflies adore flowers

Warm rain and soft wind break the chill.
With willow eyes and red plum cheeks,
I sense the heart of spring stir within.
Where is the one with whom I share
the pleasures of wine and poetry?
Streaming tears ruin my face powder,
and floral hair ornaments weigh heavily.

In my gold-embroidered robe,
I fall against a sloping hill of soft pillows,
breaking my delicate phoenix hairpins.
Embracing obscure, sorrow-laden insomnia,
one where sweet dreams fail to surface,
alone in the withering night, I trim a lamp flower.

drunk to sleep
bc she has insomnia?

Die lian hua, No. 2: Butterflies adore flowers,
    a farewell poem sent to my sister from an inn

Wet rouge and tears stain my silk dress.
I've sung four farewell verses of Yang Guan
    over a thousand times.
Long mountains and waters will separate us.
Left alone at the inn, I listen to small rains, *xiao xiao.*
Overwhelmed by grief in my reluctance to say farewell,
I forgot to share one small cup of parting wine,
a lost gesture both shallow and profound.
So I rely on this poem sent to you by messenger birds.
Still, the eastern wilderness isn't as far as paradise.

She didn't
properly say goodby
to him.

Die lian hua, No. 3: Butterflies adore flowers

Little to be desired in a long tranquil night
bearing fruitless dreams of the capital,
reminiscing about the road to Chang An.
I hear spring is especially beautiful this year,
doubled radiance of flowers and moonlight.

Though simply prepared, cups and platters
of sweet wine and tart plums are lovely,
hearty enough to satisfy the appetite.
While intoxicated, you put flowers in my hair.
Yet like silent flowers, we too are bereft of laughter
commiserating how we, like the spring, must grow old.

Haoshi jin: Incipient blessings

When wind ceases, fallen petals accumulate at depth
beyond the window blinds,
    mixing floral reds with snow.
Remember, when the crab-apple is past blooming,
spring's departure is at hand.

Wine's finished, songs are done, and jade cups, empty.
An aqua-colored lamp is dimming.
My dreams cannot harbor any more grief,
solitary cry of a nightjar.

Yi qing'er: Thoughts of Miss Qing

From a high chamber,
I survey the mountain wilderness
and rolling plains shrouded in mist.
Through miles of sparse fog,
after dark crows return to their nests,
a lone trumpet sounds in the evening.
Fragrant incense, faint perfume, is broken
by chronic bitterness, my ailing heart.
Now twilight hastens the leaves dropping
    from a parasol tree.
Yes, *wutong* leaves fall
while autumn's vivid hues flare,
yet I alone still grieve.

This grief is
Solity

38

Yuan wangsun, No. 2: Lament for the prince

Wind rises over the lake, stirs waves.
Autumn fades, red flowers thin, a rare perfume.
Light plays upon water; rugged colors of mountain
ranges evoke heartfelt passions,
and mere words fail to capture
the lovely abundance of natural creation.

Cant put into words

Ripe lotus seeds, blossoms past maturity.
Fresh dew cleanses aquatic flowers and shore grasses.
Nestled in sand, sleeping birds remain still;
        they do not turn their heads,
as if they, too, are loathe to see
a companion leave so soon.

*dont even want to
see the spring bcuz
know itll leave*

Tian zi cai sangzi: Composing lyrics
    to mulberry picking

Who planted the southern *bajiao* tree near my window?
The plantain's shadows fill my courtyard;
the *bajiao's* shadows fill the courtyard,
leaf on leaf, bud on bud, furling and unfurling
in a tender display of effervescent love.

Sorrow wets my pillow in the third night watch,
one long, ceaseless, dripping rain –
one long, ceaseless, dropping rain,
piercing the heart of this exiled northerner
rising sleepless, feckless, parted from her beloved,
unsettled by southern nocturnal sounds!

Nan gezi: Southern song

A star-laden river winds heavenward,
while in the world below, on earth,
my curtains are simply drawn;
cold pillow and sleeping mat
stained by streams of countless tears.
Rising to unfasten my silk garments,
I inquire of the night, *what is the time?*
Little lotus pods sewn against green
and gold patterns of sparse lotus leaves.
Despite cold weather like home⎞
and northern clothes to wear,⎠
this dark southern mood is not home at all!

Mai hua sheng: Voice of the flower seller

Outside the curtains, in the fifth *geng,*
night wind disperses traces of my dream.
Our library, laden with valuable books, awaits.
I remember jade pins aslant in my hair,
stoking the fire. The engraved seal burner is cold.

Our capital was violet at dusk,
the mountain peaks gold.
Now rain covers the earth with dense mist.
Rising on a spring river's current,
I wake from intoxication.
My silk collar is drenched
with a day's worth of tears.
I hear wild swans cry
on their long journey.

Yuan wangsun, No. 3: Lament for the prince

Spring comes late to the Imperial Mile.
Strong gates shield a deep garden,
lush green lawn at a stairwell.
Messenger geese cut across dusk.
Upstairs, from my living quarters,
who'll carry this letter to you?
Sorrows of eternity –
an endless cotton weave.

Passion only fuels torment,   love → loss
hard to find deliverance.
On the day of fireless remembrance,
streets, lanes, and garden swings are quiet.
A luminous white crescent rises,
soaking pear blossoms with moonlight.

Attributed to Li Qingzhao

Gan huai shi: Poem of emotions

Cold window, a broken desk without my books.
The government road led to this misery.
Qin officials love cash, the circle with a hollow square.
Meddlers bustle in droves under the winter sun.
I shut the door against callers to write a poem.
Swallows and caked fragrance fill my thoughts.
In deep solitude, I find companions
in form of birds and imaginary men.

Gu yan'er: A solitary goose

Waking in a rattan bed with paper curtains,
speechless with sorrow,
I feel bereft of poetic reflection.
Incense extinguished
in the cold jade burner,
bitterness flows like water.
A flutist plays our song three times,
"Plum Flowers in Sudden Bloom."
Our memories of spring, more or less.
Soft wind, sparse rains whisper
xiao xiao over the earth,
spilling cascades of a thousand tears.
Now the flutist departs; the jade tower, empty.
Who can share my crushed spirit?
I snap a flowering plum branch.
Between heaven and earth,
there's not one soul I can send it to.

thinks she
is all alone in
her grief

Everywhere she
looks is somewhere
he isn't.

45

Man ting fang, No. 1: A fragrant courtyard

Spring is cloistered in my little room
where a sealed window locks out the sun.
This pale space echoes profound solitude.
When the engraved incense seal dims,
dusk shadows descend the curtain hooks.
My hand-planted river plum flourishes,
so why ascend the water cascade for a view?
No one ever comes to visit.
I am lonesome as He Xun in Yang Province.
My flowering river plums are elegantly furled:
how will they survive the hapless rain,
endure the wind's harsh caresses?
In whose house does the voice of a flute
arouse rich melodic sorrows?
Fragrance will vanish, jade petals wilt
without remorse, yet their memory lingers
when the last traces are swept away.
It's hard to describe
a luminous window of sparse moonlight,
translucent shadows flowing in the wind.

Niannu jiao: A beautiful young woman

In the deserted garden
of slanting wind and thin rain,
a double gate is closed, then
lovely willows, new blossoms open
on the day of fireless remembrance.
Shifting weather distracts me.
I finish a poem's difficult rhymes,
massage my head to clear it of wine,
and savor the idle taste of pleasure.
Wild swans have flown past:
Ten thousand crises of the heart
are now too late to send by letter.
Upstairs, a few days of spring chill,
curtains drawn on all four sides.
I lean wearily against a jade rail.
The quilt's cold, incense faint
when I wake from a new dream.
Disconsolate, I rise alone,
yet fresh dew, so copious at dawn,
shimmers on the budding leaves
    of a parasol tree.
Fondly, I remember
    spring's little excursions.
As the fog lifts at high noon,
I anticipate a clear spring day.

47

Yulou chun: A jade chamber in spring
                              to the red plum flower

Red petals broken, lustrous agate buds crushed.
See whether the southern plum tips are blooming.
Refined over an undisclosed period of time,
their dormancy conceals a boundless anticipation.

At the spring window, a nun wears a distressed spirit.
Weathering a thousand sorrows, she doesn't venture
on the landing or lean over the balustrade for air.
The more our plum flowers invite her to look, however,
the more they fade, withering swiftly, though
by tomorrow morning, the wind may not even arise.

Zhegu tien, No. 2: A partridge sky

7. xiao xiao

Winter wind whispers *xiao xiao*
as the ice sun climbs a sealed window;
a wide-leafed parasol tree
loathes incipient night frost;
a drop of wine commends
the fragrant bitterness of tea,
and a camphor aroma of incense
    breaks my dream.
Autumn fades swiftly
though the days feel endless.
As Zhong Xuan lived far from home, in exile,
I dwell in the cold depths of seclusion.
Why not be content with one's measure, a cup of wine,
never to lose the yellow hearts of chrysanthemums
flourishing by the eastern fence.

49

Qingping yue: Song of peace

Annually, in the snow,
I would gather plum flowers, intoxicated
by their scent, caressing the petals
until my clothes were drenched
    with fresh spring tears.

This year, after journeying far
    between heaven and earth,
I notice my hair silvering at the temples.
With the increasing boldness of twilight wind,
I know the sight of plum flowers
    will soon be rare.

Chun chan (shi): Spring fades

When spring fades, a bittersweet nostalgia
    arises for home.
During the illness, I loathe brushing my long hair.
Under the beams, swallows chatter
    the whole winter day.
Sparse wind fills the blinds with a fragrance of roses.

doesnt wrote to
set up

51

Sheng zhazi, guiqing: Searching for passions
   in the women's chamber

Year on year in the jade mirror,
I look at my plum blossom rouge,
counting the years he's failed to return.
Fearful of a letter from south of the river,
flooding my heart without wine, I weep.
Quietly I imagine the remote mists of tropical forests.
My beloved husband is so far,
the sky's margin is close by compare.

[handwritten annotation] her husband
is further than
the sky

Tanpo huan xi sha, No. 2: Long variation
   on sands of a silk-washing stream

After the illness, the hair on my forehead silvered.
As I lay quietly, a faint moon rose
   up the window screen.
Perfumed cardamom sprouts simmered in water,
a scent indistinguishable from hot tea.
The poetry books on my pillow helped to pass the time.
Outside my door, new autumn rain refreshed the soul.
You spent the whole day facing me, refined grace –
fragrant osmanthus flower.

rain = good?

Lin jiang xien, No. 2: Immortals gaze at the river

The lush courtyard rests in abundant depth,
windows clouded with mist,
inner rooms shut in by fog
as willows tips and plum calyxes
    slowly come to life.
As spring returns to the trees of Mo Ling,
my health declines in this southern city.

Singing of wind and moonlight,
    sundry matters now past,
I've come of age without success.
Who cares for this tattered woman,
    withered to nothing,
lighting the lamp without emotion,
treading on snow without sympathy.

Old new

Yong yule: Eternal bliss

The dropping sun is liquid gold.
Dusk clouds, a jade pendant.
Where is my beloved in this world?
Unthinned mist dyes the willows.
A solitary flute plays
the lament of plum flowers.
Countless spring thoughts
arrive with the Lantern Festival,
days of fair weather followed
by ineluctable wind and rain.
Friends summon me
with their fragrant vehicles,
beautiful, well-bred horses.
Politely, I decline invitations
to our wine and poetry circle.
In the opulent days of the lost capital,
I relished leisure in the women's chamber.
The Lantern Festival was my favorite. *"wes"*
Ornate emerald hair accessories,
snow-willow pins of delicate gold,
dressed in elegant, decorative sashes,
how we competed extravagantly.
Now I am a withered woman
with wind-blown, frost-white hair.
Reluctant to venture out at night, *wont leave; jut*
I remain a recluse behind lowered blinds, *listens*
listening to laughter and conversation.

I've written poetry for thirty years,
sealed my lips, and shunned fame.
Now this man raves about my poetry
like the irritating name-dropping scholar
who spoke to everyone of the hermit poet,
Xiang Si.

Shes writing
from experience
place.
She feels like this
is painting her
coping method
that way for her, not
to join her a room

Yujia ao, No. 2: A fisherman's pride

When the sky, mist, and waved clouds mingle at dawn,
when a star-laden river, the Milky Way, wheels
   in the dance of a thousand sails,
then my spirit, in a dream, drifts to the empyrean,
listening to heaven's voice
gently asking me about a journey:
   What is your desire?
I answer with a sigh: The road is long at dusk;
I've studied poetry intently,
   even written a few startling lines.
Yet the powerful *peng* bird
   soars high for ninety thousand *li*
   on pure wind, unceasing wind,
as I desire to send my little boat
   three mythic mountains away.

Her feeling
disassociated from the
world around her

Xiao meng (shi): Sunrise dream

Dawn, in a dream, at the sound of bells,
I stepped lightly on low rose-hued clouds,
stood in the presence of An Qishen
and met the immortal woman, Ou Luhua.
A shifting autumn wind dispersed
celestial flowers in a jade well.
I witnessed lotus roots tall as ships
and consumed sweet dates large as gourds.
Seated on a flying lotus flower,
I heard witty, clever exchanges,
engaged in sophisticated conversation,
and shared fresh tea, the fire of life.
Though my adventure may not
accomplish the emperor's tasks,
it creates boundless joy within.
All should live as such from birth.
Yearning for my former home,
I rise in the morning, pick up clothes,
and cover my ears against the din.
Though I may never return,
I find solace, with a sigh, in a dream.

had a · joyful dream

Man ting fang, No. 2: A fragrant courtyard

Fragrant wild grasses flourish by the pond,
lovely green shadows fill the courtyard,
a late chill penetrates the window screen.
Jade curtain hooks and gold locks,
a lone flute's song, and rare visitors:
Alone at the table before cups of wine,
I brood over endless sorrows
flowing from sea to sky, the horizon.
How can I live without you?
The summer rose has withered,
so I rely on pear blossoms for solace.
We loved one another through the years:
Fresh perfume drenched my sleeves;
we drank the tea of fiery passion,
witnessed pageants of horses, festivals
where lightweight riverboats raced.
Fearless in face of violent storms,
we raised our wine to crushed petals.
Now I wonder
why those days have fled.
I await your return.

Ce 1

Jin shi lu, houxu: Records on Metal and Stone

Epilogue

The purpose of this epilogue is to discuss a chronicle written by my late husband, Zhao Mingcheng. Initially, my lord composed this book of thirty scrolls to describe the rubbings of stone and metal inscriptions in our collection of antiquities.

When my husband was twenty-one, he was a student at the national university. Although we were both raised in erudite families, the Zhao and Lee clans, we embraced a frugal ethic and lived simply. Every half month or so, my husband would visit his family. After pawning his clothes for half a thousand coins, he would take a walk to the market at Xiang Guo monastery to buy fruit and *beiwen* or stone rubbings. When he returned home, we would compare the treasures he purchased, opening the scrolls to admire them while eating fruit. We were so happy, filled with simple contentment, we compared ourselves to subjects who lived with austere grace under emperor He Tian. After two years, when my husband was appointed to a government post, he journeyed expediently to and fro under the sky, collecting ancient writings and unique calligraphy. Our modest collection of antiquities grew until it included rare collectibles and quality editions by famous literati.

Once, a man offered to sell us a painting of peonies by Xu Xi for the price of two hundred thousand copper coins. Although we realized that even wealthy aristocrats could not afford it, we took the scroll home to admire for a couple nights before returning it to the seller. Afterward, as husband and wife, we faced one another with profound sadness at the loss of such a treasure.

In later years, when we lived in a rural setting, my husband was appointed over two prefectures, one after another. We stretched our humble provisions and lived by modest means, spending enough for basic sustenance like food and clothing. We continued to indulge in our favorite hobby of collecting antiquities, however, acquiring new books and comparing them to other editions before adding them to our collection. Whenever we obtained a new text, we would spend the entire day discussing it, opening a famous scroll or holding up a rare piece, critiquing each new specimen with outstretched fingers. We indicated flaws or errata until one burning candle dimmed and extinguished. Our entire collection of ancient papers, letters, calligraphy, and paintings was impressive in quality and scope.

Eventually, to support our expensive hobby, <u>I gave up wearing elaborate hair ornaments adorned with pearls</u> and omitted the second course of my meals. Sitting together in Gui Lai Gong, the Homecoming Hall, we drank tea and sorted piles of fine books. My husband and I played a game where books were opened at random and the person who could name the book, chapter, page, and line would have the privilege of drinking his or her tea first. Whenever I won, I would raise my cup with a hearty laugh, often spilling the tea on myself before I could drink my winner's cup.

When we were satisfied with the extent of our book collection, we built an archive to store the volumes. In the year of Jing Kang, when my husband was working as a government official in Zi Chuan prefecture, he heard the northern invaders had conquered the capital. In dismay, we looked around at our boxes, chests, cases, and trunks overflowing with precious books, overwhelmed with adoration and desire mingled with profound remorse at their imminent loss.

In the Ding Wei year, my husband left for the south after his mother passed away. By then, our collection of books and antiquities was too heavy to transport. First, we laid aside the heavy print volumes, then large paintings with multiple sections, and metal antiques without engravings. Next we set aside the less valuable editions of books, literally run-of-the-mill paintings, and cumbersome bronze vessels. After all this sorting, we still had fifteen vehicles loaded with artifacts from our collection which crossed the Huai River in a commissioned string of connected boats.

At our old home in Qing Province, we left ten locked rooms filled with objects from our collection, hoping to carry them away next year by boat. Tragically, all our possessions were destroyed, burned to ash by northern invaders. In the sixth month, my husband and I lived temporarily on the river. As he prepared to leave for his next government post, he looked into the center of our boat with a grave, solitary air. I felt quite despondent. I asked him what to do if I heard of any trouble in the city. He responded, first toss away the domestic goods, then the clothes, books and scrolls, and then the antique vessels. Take the ancestral sacrificial urns with you and run with them, carrying them yourself. Don't forget this, he said, and rode away on his horse.

Later, in the autumn, during the eighth month, I received the dreadful news that my husband had fallen ill and couldn't rise from his bed. At the time, he was staying at an inn. I sailed west on our river boat to find him. Shortly after I arrived, he passed away. After the funeral, I was left alone. That winter, I had planned to live with in-laws in Hong Province. The very same winter, however, Hong Province was captured, falling to the northern invaders. Our valuable collection, which once crossed a river in a string of boats, was dispersed like clouds and smoke. I was alone in the world without a husband and without material possessions. All that remained were a few little scrolls and some books by Li Bai, Du Fu, Han Yu, and Liu Zongyuan, *Collected Stories of the World* and *Discussions on Salt and Iron*, rubbings of stone inscriptions, around a dozen antique tripods, and about ten chests or boxes of items from the Southern Tang period. This was all that survived of the possessions I stored safely during my own illness after my husband's, when I stayed indoors continually, in the lying-down room.

At this time, I couldn't travel upstream on the river because of the northern invaders. Moreover, when I arrived in Tai Province, the prefect had already fled, and the court released all its government officials.

65

Previously, when my husband was ill, a distinguished visitor presented us with a jade nephrite vase as a gift. In the spring, however, when the government subdued some mutinous troops, the vase ended up in the late General Li's house, not to mention other possessions from our collection of antiquities.

Now fifty to sixty percent of the surviving collection had completely disappeared. In sum, only five to seven baskets and trunks of calligraphy materials and paintings remained with me when I was staying with the Zhong family. One evening, a thief stole five bamboo trunks. In despair, I offered a generous financial reward for their return. Despite all my efforts to recover what survived of our collection, I failed to retrieve most of the stolen books and expository writings.

As I look through this chronicle, it is as though my late husband meets me again in the Hall of Jing Zhi in Dong Lai. I remember how he would label the books and bind them carefully, constructing a cover for each. In the evenings, he would write an epilogue for one scroll in each pair. Of these two thousand scrolls, five hundred and twenty scrolls have epilogues handwritten by my husband. Indeed, the work of my husband's hands appears fresh, even though the trees planted on his grave are tall with the passing of years.

Through these experiences, I am familiar with the woes of amassing wealth and watching it dispersed, cycles of loss and gain. Such cycles are part of universal human existence. In hindsight, I return to the small, rather trivial curios acquired in the arc of my husband's life from beginning to end. I warn those who read this epilogue, those who aspire to collect antiquities and elegant artifacts, and the erudite who desire to pursue happiness: This is what I have learned about life.

Xiao Yi ignored the collapse of the dynasty and destroyed his library collections. Yang Guang did not mourn his own death, but rather, returned in spirit to retrieve his possessions. Detailed, complete, and thorough, this chronicle bears a testimony to those who read its words. I do hope readers will learn from my experiences, understanding the transience of materialism which may bring joy lasting only a season, leaving the acquisitive more sorrowful than ever before.

Afterthoughts

In my thirty-four years of life since the age of eighteen, when I married my husband, up to the present day, I fretted endlessly about the acquisition and retention of valuables. I've experienced the loss of an extensive collection of antiquities. My late husband invested much time and effort in documenting thousands of items which are now dispersed, utterly irretrievable.

I write this epilogue so that others might receive edification.

68

69

AFTERWORD

Li Qingzhao (1084 – ca. 1151), one of China's leading classical women poets, was born in Shandong during the Song Dynasty (960-1279), according to Kang-I Sun Chang and Haun Saussy in *Women Writers of Traditional China*. Raised in an elite family, she married Zhao Mingcheng, the son of a high-ranking government official. Her distinctly woman-centered sensibility focuses on subjects of marital love, exile, and war with emotional and allusive depth. As evident in her writings, she was deeply in love with her husband Zhao, who shared her aesthetic interests and often appears in her poems. Together, she and her husband collected art and literature. Li and Zhao co-authored an extensive catalogue of artifacts, *Records on Metal and Stone*, for which Li wrote an epilogue on war and exile. Indeed, Li's tranquil life of writing and art-collecting was inevitably susceptible to the political instabilities of her time. After the fall of the Northern Song Dynasty, she and Zhao were forced to abandon their treasured possessions as they fled into southern exile. Subsequently, Li lost her beloved spouse to a fatal illness during one of his relocations to a new government post. On their journeys, most of their art collection was stolen or reduced to ash.

Though widely circulated in her lifetime, Li's six-volume oeuvre was dispersed after her death. Her voice surfaces in clustered poems preserved by classical anthologies in the ensuing centuries. I first came across Li's work in Dorothy Disse's on-line treasury, *Other Women's Voices*. Whether Li recalls a youthful boating excursion with joy, observes a courtyard plantain tree flourishing in her southern exile, listens to rain dripping from the wide leaves of a parasol tree, watches for the first signs of yellow chrysanthemums, recalls her late husband with tender regret—her hair silvering at the temples—or sits quietly with a burning censer after dusk, her lyrics resonate with compassion for all that's lost and redeemed in this life or thereafter.

While Li's poems of youth celebrate marital love and the joys of nature, the poems composed in her later years voice the painful trials of war. Her epilogue to *Records on Metal and Stone*, a commentary upon the vast collection of scrolls, vessels, paintings, and other cultural artifacts she and Zhao collected, offers insight to her experiences with war and exile, meditating upon losses and gains in the cycle of life. Likewise, the intimate nature of her poetry appeals to general readerships, setting Li apart from classical women poets who chose more stylized approaches, and apart from those poets, male or female, who sought to work within patriotic or morally didactic trends framed by imperial culture. Li selected a lyric style, *ci*—one historically authored by men, though sung and performed by women—to voice her subjectivity. Moreover, by alluding to renowned poets such as Qu Yuan, she positions herself within a distinguished literary heritage while using a woman-centered lyric "I." Writing about the personal, she also voices timeless truth: themes of love, memory, and exile are universal to human experience.

A few notes on Li's oeuvre: According to Chang and Saussy, only about fifty *ci*, a handful of *shi*, and a couple prose pieces survive today of her original six-volume collection. In the table of contents, *shi* or traditional poems are noted as such; the rest of the poems are *ci*, a short lyric form. One of Li's favorite poetic modes of expression, *ci* were songs with titles such as "*Rumeng ling:* As if a reverie," "*Huan xi sha:* Sands of a silk-washing stream," and "*Yujia ao:* A proud fisherman." Translators commonly include the prefix "To the Tune of . . ." to the *ci* songs which Li used for composing her poems. Originally sung by female musicians in the imperial court, *ci* were composed predominantly by male literati, even when subjects and personae in the lyrics were women. A number of *ci* survive today with the attribution, "anonymous," which scholars Beata Grant and Wilt Idema propose were women. As noted in Grant and Idema's anthology, *The Red Brush: Writing Women of Imperial China*, the popular *ci* developed into a significant literary genre when it shifted from a class of "low art" performed by female courtesans to "high art" composed by literati such as Li Qingzhao. Although the actual melodies to the songs are now lost, their formal structures still remain; the *ci* form prescribed metrical patterns, rhyme schemes, and even word tones.

Arranging this selection of Li's poetry and prose, I hope to convey a sense of progression from the bliss of her youth through trials of war, allowing a sense of transformation through the years. Among the tasks facing translators of classical Chinese poetry are lyric elisions and resonant allusions; elegant internal and end-stopped rhymes, homonyms and homophones, and the visual qualities of Chinese ideograms present the translator with challenges in degrees of equivalence. I focused on rendering the music and meaning of Li Qingzhao's works with a hope of conveying their original dynamic beauty. To this end, these translations capture her allusions, passionate imagery—corporeal yet ethereal—and elegant restraint without too many liberties, creating an eloquent English echo for a readership encountering her work centuries later.

The courtyard glows with fragrant torches
in the spring wind, shining effulgence.

Li Qingzhao

NOTES

One controversial biographical detail concerns Li Qingzhao's second marriage after Zhao's death, initially disputed by neo-Confucian scholars who, in the context of Confucian ethics, found the widowed Li's decision to marry and divorce a second husband implausible for an eminent woman of her era. Since a poet's writings were considered the fruit of her moral virtues, scholars preferred to believe that a renowned poet like Li would follow prescribed ethics in her own life. However, as literary historians Beata Grant and Wilt Idema elucidate, Li's contemporaries were widely aware of her second marriage, and translator Ling Chung states that it was not unusual for widows to remarry in the Song Dynasty. The primary piece of evidence for the divorce is Li's letter to a distant relative, Qi Chongli, referring clearly to the second marriage. Others argue it is a forgery, while scholars Haun Saussy and Kang-I Sun Chang refer to the story as a legend. The letter describes the pain Li experienced in her second marriage, including references to the man's abusive behavior. She expresses profound regret about marrying him. Ronald C. Egan, in fact, argues that traditional criticism erroneously interprets Li's oeuvre as autobiographical; on the contrary, a gender bias arose to suit cultural norms. Apart from the letter, details of Li's later years are sparse. Since she was childless, it is likely that she lived with her brother, a government official, and enjoyed a
quiet life of solitude.

Of course, she continued to write poems.

For discussions on Li's possible second marriage and divorce, see Grant & Idema (p. 216) and Chang & Saussy (p. 89). For literary and historical information on Li Qingzhao, see Grant & Idema (pp. 204–207) and Chang & Saussy (p. 89). Please also refer to Egan's monograph, *The Burden of Female Talent*, which sheds an alternate light.

A note on literary form: Translators commonly include the prefix "To the Tune of . . ." to the *ci* songs which Li used for composing her poems. Since I mentioned this fact in the introduction, I chose to omit prefixes in the translations. Grant & Idema include a description of *ci* as a literary form and provide a translation of Li's critical essay on *ci*, "Cilun" (pp. 217-8, 220).

Rumeng ling, No. 2: As if a reverie
"Screen-rolling servant" refers to Li's servant, who is unrolling a bed-curtain (a literal "screen"), rousing Li from sleep. Concerned about the crab apple's petals after a nocturnal rainstorm, Li anxiously queries the servant, who assumes the "tree is as always." Li's response in the last lines are literally translated as: "The green is fat and the red is thin," referring to an abundance green leaves while frail red flowers are sparse.

Huan xi sha, No. 1: Sands of a silk-washing stream
A confession to the reader: As a poet-translator, I took liberties in this poem. In lines 1 and 8: "lion-hued" and "red–embered happiness" are not grammatically present in Li's original. "Lion-hued" is based on the resonances of "hu" which shares a part of the ideogram for lion and for vessel or cup, a homophonic, paranomastic play on words. The red embers of a burning candle wick are considered auspicious in a poetic context – symbolizing a good omen. Instead of relegating these rich harmonies to the endnotes, I amplified the translation.

Huan xi sha, No. 3: Sands of a silk-washing stream
The day of s remembrance refers to "Cold Food Day," when no cooking fires are lit. Cold food is eaten to commemorate Jie Zitui, a high-ranking state official who was accidentally burned to death by the emperor (Chang & Saussy pp. 92-93). In line 6, "hill-pillow" is a porcelain headrest with a round opening where Li keeps her little hairpins. The last two lines of the poem may be alternately translated as "then yellow dusk falls with soft light rain / upon the lone garden swing."

Huan xi sha, No. 4: Sands of a silk-washing stream
The bright rhinoceros horn may refer to a cup of wine or to the medicinal use of ground rhinoceros horn.

Tanpo huan xi sha, No. 1: Long variation on sands of a silk-washing stream Yen Fu, Director of the Imperial Secretariat during the Western Jin Dynasty (265-316 AD), was known for his brilliant charisma (Chang & Saussy p. 96).

Guifei ge (shi): Imperial consort's chamber
According to Ling Chung, Guifei does not refer specifically to the famous Tang Dynasty consort, Yang Guifei. Rather, the phrase is a title for the first-ranking imperial consort. Gou Yi is the name of the Han Dynasty palace, residence of Emperor Wu's consort, also called Gou Yi. She gave birth to a son, heir to the throne (Chung p. 115).

Zhegu tien, No. 1: A partridge sky for the cassia flower
Qu Yuan (c. 340 BC - 278 BC) was a high-ranking state official and poet during the Warring States Period (475–221 BC). Chrysanthemums were his favorite flower.

Yujia ao, No. 1: A proud fisherman
Green-ants wine, according to Lu-sheng Chong, produces a green froth or vapor when poured (p. 2).

Xiari jue ju: Broken lines under a summer sun
Xiang Yu was a heroic general of the Qin Dynasty (221–207 BC) (Grant & Idema p. 241).

Ti Bayonglou: Composed for the tower of eight poems
The tower of eight poems, *Bayonglou,* was built for Shen Yueh, a fifth century poet, critic, and prefect (Chung p. 113).

Duoli, yong baiju: Quite beautiful, a song for the white chrysanthemum
This poem contains several historical and literary allusions. Gui Fei is Yang Guifei, the Tang Dynasty consort whose relationship with the emperor ended fatally with the downfall of the regime. When intoxicated, her face would turn red as a peony (Chung p. 99). According to Lu-sheng Chong's notes, Sun Shou was a general's wife who drew attention to the beauty of her melancholy eyebrows (p. 2). Han Ling had an affair with the daughter of a high-ranking court official and received a gift of stolen incense from her. The incense, stolen from the young woman's father, scented Han Ling's gown and brought the affair to light (Chung p. 99). The woman from Xu is emperor Liang Yuandi's consort Xu Zhaopei, who powdered only half her face to deride the one-eyed emperor (Chung p. 15, 99). Tao Ling was a mayor of Pengze who gathered chrysanthemums by the eastern hedge (Chong p. 3). The young women in Han Gao (northwest of Xiangyang, Hubei Province) greeted a young man, Zheng Jiafu, who asked for their jade ornaments. The women complied. When Zheng looked again, however, the women and jade ornaments had vanished (Chong p. 5). Ban Zhao was a disposed consort who inscribed a poem on a white silk fan and sent it to the emperor. The poem describes the silk fan's fear of autumn, when it will be forgotten in a bamboo chest (Chong p. 6).

Dian jiang chun: Applying lip rouge
In some versions, the word "fang" (perfumed) is used in the second to last line; in others, "xuai" (dry and withered) is used.

Zuihua yin: Intoxicated by floral shadows
Chong Yang refers to the chrysanthemum-adorned Double Nine festival (Grant & Idema p. 230; p. 94 Chang & Saussy).

Wuling chun: Wuling spring
"Coupled rivers" in line 2 of the second stanza may also be translated as "Paired Rivers," a town in Zhejiang province where two rivers merge.

Fenghuang tai shang yi chiu xiao:
Playing the flute on the phoenix terrace, a memory
"Wuling beloved" is a poetic reference to Li's husband, Zhao. Li compares him to the Wuling fisherman who, according to lore, discovers a faraway utopia in a peach orchard (Chong p. 3).

Xing xiangzi, qi xi: Fragrance in motion, seven dusks
The story of the cattle hand and weaver maiden is one of celestial love. After the weaver maiden and cattle hand fall deeply love, they abandon their duties and offend the immortals with their constant lovemaking. Subsequently, they are turned into constellations and placed at opposite ends of the sky. Once a year, magpies form a bridge so the couple can meet.

Die lian hua, No. 1: Butterflies adore flowers
In the last line, "deng hua" is literally translated as "lamp flower," and refers to a burning wick.

Die lian hua, No. 2: Butterflies adore flowers, a farewell poem
    sent to my sister from an inn
Yang Guan, or "Yang Pass," is a farewell song. According to Grant & Idema, it originates from a poem by Tang Dynasty poet Wang Wei, "Sending Mr. Yuan on his way on a mission to Anxi" (p. 226).

Die lian hua, No. 3: Butterflies adore flowers
Chang An was the capital of the Tang Dynasty. It also refers to the lost northern Song Dynasty capital, Kai Feng (Chung p. 102). The line, "doubled radiance of flowers and moonlight," is translated more literally but awkwardly as, "flower glow moon scene truly one another reflect," approximated by this following paraphrase, which includes the subtle connotations of *reflect*: "the light of flowers and moonlit scene truly shine upon each other to complement one another."

Yi qing'er: Thoughts of Miss Qing

Two words are missing in the original. In the ninth line of the translation, in the absence of the original words, I added, "Now twilight."

Mai hua sheng: Voice of the flower seller
One "geng" is a watch of the night. The night is divided into five geng or night watches.

Zhegu tien, No. 2: A partridge sky
Zhong Xuan, who lived in exile, was a poet of the third century who fled the Han court after its downfall (Chung p. 102).

Yong yule: Eternal bliss
The Lantern Festival is celebrated with paper lanterns at the end of the Chinese New Year.

Fende zhi ziyun: Singled out by the poetry circle
The name-dropping man refers to a high-ranking court official, Yang Qingzi, who showered accolades upon Xiang Si, a hermit poet of the ninth century (Chung p. 117).

Yujia ao, No. 2: A fisherman's pride
The peng, notes Lu-sheng Chong, is a mythic bird. On its half-year journey to the southern ocean, the peng flies over the sea for three thousand *li*, then soars on the wind to ninety thousand *li* (p. 2).

Xiao meng: Sunrise dream
An Qishan and Ou Luhua are mythic immortals of wisdom (Chung p. 117).

Jin shi lu, houxu: Records on metal and stone, epilogue
Li Qingzhao wrote this epilogue to her husband Zhao's thirty-scroll book, *Jin shi lu.* The book chronicles their estimated two thousand bronze and stone rubbings. Li's epilogue, which uses traits of an autobiographical essay, shares personal insights to her happy marriage, tragic separations from her husband in war and exile, and philosophical reflections on loss and gain. Grant & Idema's translation, "Inscriptions on Bronze and Stone," mentions that Li and Zhao's collection spans the Three Dynasties (Xia 2207-1766 B.C., Shang or Yin 1765 – 1122 B.C., and Zhou 1121 – 249 B.C.) to the Five Dynasties (rulers in Northern China, 907-960 A.D.). It further mentions that Li Qingzhao's father was vice-director in the Ministry of Rites; Li's father-in-law, Zhao's father, was vice-minister in the Ministry of Personnel (p. 208). Grant & Idema's translation also includes an italicized post-note to the epilogue: "*Written in the Studio of*

Simple Peace, on the first day of the Eighth Month of the second year, a ren *year, of the reign period Continued Restoration"* (p. 214).

REFERENCES

Chang, Kang-i Sun and Haun Saussy. *Women Writers of Traditional China: An Anthology of Poetry and Criticism.* Palo Alto, CA: Stanford University Press, 2000. Print.

Chao, Lucy. "Complete Collection of Ci by Li Qingzhao." 25 September 2006.
<http://www.chinapage.com/liqing-poetry.html>. Web.

Chong, Lu-sheng. "Chinese Cultural Learning Center." Gonzaga University. 22 August 2001. 25 September 2006.
<http://barney.gonzaga.edu/~chongls/toc2.htm>. Web.

Disse, Dorothy. "Li Qingzhao (c. 1083 – aft. 1149)." *Other Women's Voices: Translations of Women's Writing before 1700.* 1 January 2009. 22 December 2005.
<http://home.infionline.net/~ddisse/liquinzh.html>. Web.

Egan, Ronald C. *The Burden of Female Talent.* Cambridge, MA: Harvard University Press, 2014. Print.

Grant, Beata and Wilt Idema. *The Red Brush: Writing Women of Imperial China.* Cambridge, MA: Harvard East Asian Monographs, 2004. Print.

Li Ch'ing-chao. *Complete Poems.* Kenneth Rexroth and Ling Chung, translators and editors. New York: New Directions, 1979. Print.

Ming-Qing Women's Writings Digitization Project. Yenching Library. Cambridge, MA: Harvard University. 2005.
<http://digital.library.mcgill.ca/mingqing/english/index.htm>
Web.

GRATEFUL ACKNOWLEDGEMENTS

I am not the first translator of Li's work, nor the last. In addition to the fine work of scholars Beata Grant and Wilt Idema, I am grateful to Lucy Chao, Kang-I Sun Chang, Ling Chung, Lu-sheng Chong, and Haun Saussy for their valuable historical and biographical notes on Li Qingzhao's writings. I first encountered Li Qingzhao while perusing Dorothy Disse's on-line archive, *Other Women's Voices: Translations of Women's Writing before 1700*. Arthur Sze has also eloquently translated a number of Li's poems. I express appreciation for the Ming-Qing Women's Writings Digitization Project at the Yenching Library of Harvard University, which provided on-line access to anthologized originals. Lucy Chao and Lu-Sheng Chong also provided source-language texts with insightful commentary. Heartfelt thanks to Chao, Chong, and Disse for their digital treasuries of Li's poetry.

Last but not least, I am grateful to the following publications, wherein my translations first appeared in slightly altered form.

Circumference Magazine: Poetry in Translation
To the Tune of *Xing Xiangzi, Qi Xi*: Fragrance in motion, seven dusks
To the Tune of *Yi Jian Mei*: Cutting a plum flower branch
To the Tune of *Yu Jia Ao*: A fisherman's pride (as "A lofty fisherman")

Michigan Quarterly Review, University of Michigan
Dian jiang chun: Applying lip rouge
Wuling chun: Wuling spring
Fenghuang tai shang yi chui xiao:
      Playing the flute on the phoenix terrace

Shadows & Echoes, Pacific Lutheran University
Haoshi jin: Incipient Blessings, *Qingping yue:* Song of peace,
Tanpo huan xi sha 1: Long variation on sands of a silk-washing stream
Tanpo huan xi sha 2: Long variation on sands of a silk-washing stream
Yi qing'er: Thoughts of Miss Qing
Yuan wangsun 2: Lament for the prince

ABOUT THE TRANSLATOR

Karen An-hwei Lee is the author of *Phyla of Joy* (Tupelo 2012), *Ardor* (Tupelo 2008) and *In Medias Res* (Sarabande 2004), winner of the Norma Farber First Book Award. She authored a novel, *Sonata in K* (Ellipsis 2017). Lee also wrote two chapbooks, *God's One Hundred Promises* (Swan Scythe 2002) and *What the Sea Earns for a Living* (Quaci Press 2014). Her book of literary criticism, *Anglophone Literatures in the Asian Diaspora: Literary Transnationalism and Translingual Migrations* (Cambria 2013), was selected for the Cambria Sinophone World Series. Lee's work appears in literary journals such as *The American Poet, Poetry, Kenyon Review, Gulf Coast, IMAGE: Art, Faith, Mystery, Journal of Feminist Studies & Religion, Iowa Review,* and *Columbia Poetry Review* and was recognized by the *Prairie Schooner* / Glenna Luschei Award. She earned an M.F.A. from Brown University and Ph.D. in English from the University of California, Berkeley. The recipient of a National Endowment for the Arts Grant, Lee is a voting member of the National Book Critics Circle. Currently, she lives in San Diego and serves in the university administration at Point Loma Nazarene University.

Made in the USA
Middletown, DE
19 August 2023

36994855R00060